Conceived and produced by
Lionheart Books
10 Chelmsford Square
London NW10 3AR

Editor: Lionel Bender
Designer: Ben White
Assistant Editor: Madeleine Samuel

First published in Great Britain in 1988 by
Macdonald & Co (Publishers) Ltd
Greater London House
Hampstead Road
London NW1 7QX

Macdonald & Co Ltd, London & Sydney
A Pergamon Press plc company

Printed in Belgium

British Library Cataloguing in Publication Data
McKie, Robin
    Energy.
    1. Energy – For children
    I. Title
    531'.6
ISBN 0-356-13636-1
ISBN 0-356-16442-X Pbk
Illustrations by Hayward Art Group,
except pages 16–17, 24–25, 32–33 and 40–41,
by James G. Robins

Make up: Radius

Picture credits
Pages as numbered. T=top, C=centre, B=bottom, L=left, R=right. [Science Photo Library (SPL), Energy Technology Visuals Collection, US Dept of Energy (ETVC)]
5: Lowell Georgia/SPL, 6: David Austen/Bruce Coleman Ltd, 8: Prof. D. O. Hall, 9: A Shell Photo, 10: Philippe Plailly/SPL, 11T: A Shell Photo, 11C: Heine Schneebeli/SPL, 11B: A Shell Photo, 12T: Canada House, 12B: ZEFA, 13: Kvaerner Brug, 14T: ETSU, UK Dept of Energy, 14B: Simon Fraser/SPL, 15T: ETVC, 15B: Cambourne School of Mines, 18T: Precision Visuals/SPL, 18B: Ocean Drilling Program, Texas A&M University, 19T: Canada House, 19BL: ETVC, 19BR: Avna Dia, 20BL: Heine Schneebeli/SPL, 20TR: Pete Addis, 20BR: British Coal, 21T: ETVC, 21CR,BL: British Coal, 22L: M. Brigaud/EDF, 22R: British Nuclear Fuels plc, 23L: CEA, 23R: Scandia National Labs/SPL, 26B: Lawrence Livermore Lab/SPL, 26–27: Richard Matthews/Planet Earth Pictures, 27L: British Petroleum, 27R: Lawrence Migdale/SPL, 28T: NSHEB, 28B: ZEFA, 29T: Peter Fraenkel, 29BL: Photosonics/ETVC, 29BR: London Brick Landfill, 30T,B: ETVC, 31B: Prof. D. O. Hall, 31T: Pete Addis, 34: Adam Hart-Davis/SPL, 35TL: Photosonics/ETVC, 35TR: SPL, 35B: Dr Oviatt, Rhode Island Univ., 36B: ETVC, 36C: UKAEA, 37BR: ASEA-Atom, 37TR: ETVC, 37BR: UKAEA, 38T: Energy Inform Ltd, 38B: Pete Addis, 39: Prof. D. O. Hall, 42: Bramaz/ZEFA, 43 and Cover: ETVC.

Cover photo: Particle Beam Fusion Accelerator, Sandia National Laboratory, New Mexico.

Photo opposite: Solar power reflector tower, Edison, California.

SCIENCE FRONTIERS

ROBIN McKIE

Macdonald

ABOUT THIS BOOK

Science Frontiers reviews the current state of scientific research and development in the major areas of technology. It sets out to show what scientists, inventors and designers are trying to achieve, and to explain why their work is so important. Why, for example, in Energy are geologists digging down deep into the Earth's crust? What do physicists hope to achieve by bombarding atoms with laser beams? How can we harness the energy produced by geysers or by microscopic creatures?

This book is divided into four sections – Energy all around, Basic energy, New sources and Coping with energy. Each describes the major trends in a particular field of energy science and technology, and then looks in more detail at selected examples of research and development. The stories are illustrated throughout with photographs and diagrams. The final part of each section projects current trends forwards, and shows how settings such as coal and shale mines, and energy-efficient farms and towns, might look in the year 2001.

At the end of the book, What Next? looks a little beyond 2001. The glossary provides definitions of technical words used in the text.

△ Geothermal powered electricity generation plant, New Zealand.

CONTENTS

INTRODUCTION

Energy technology is a relatively new science. Until about 150 years ago, before the Industrial Revolution, demand for energy was satisfied largely by local supplies of wood, coal and power from watermills and windmills. As demand for power for machines increased, so scientists were encouraged to experiment with new forms of energy production, such as oil, hydro-electric and nuclear power. Then, in the 1970s came the international Oil Crisis. This saw a dramatic increase in the price of crude oil. Not only did the economy of Western countries suffer, but non-developed (Third World) countries fell further behind in their standard of living – they could not meet the higher costs of energy.

Since the Oil Crisis, scientists all over the world have experimented with and researched into all possible ways of producing energy. They have also been forced to look at the side-effects of burning coal, oil and gas – the fossil fuels – and of storing nuclear waste. Often this has involved looking at alternative sources of energy and re-examining old methods.

The following pages present a selection of the latest ideas, designs and inventions created as solutions to these problems.

▽ Dung cakes for sale in India. In much of the Third World, dung from farm animals is left to dry then burnt as fuel.

▷ Drilling for oil in Nigeria. Today, oil accounts for 95 per cent of Nigeria's income from abroad, much of it from western nations.

8

THE SUN

The Sun is the most abundant source of energy available to us. Solar energy equivalent to burning 500,000 billion barrels of oil enters our atmosphere every year, though some of this is absorbed by clouds. Nevertheless, the same amount of solar energy reaches the ground in an hour as we consume as fuel in a year.

Unfortunately, making use of this gift from Nature is difficult, for although plentiful, sunlight is not very hot. Scientists are now developing ways to concentrate solar energy. Firstly, there are collectors. These are mirrors that focus the Sun's rays on to water tanks which are heated to generate steam and run turbines. Photovoltaic cells – the other main type of generator – turn sunlight directly into electricity. Both systems have different uses.

▼ DISHES AND TOWERS

Exploiting solar energy can be difficult because the Sun continually moves across the sky. Mirrors must be designed so they can be aimed at the Sun accurately to collect the maximum amount of energy and also to follow its path with pinpoint precision. This was a difficult undertaking, until computers and heat sensors were developed to do the tasks automatically.

Some solar collectors are dish-shaped and focus the Sun's rays on to a central mirror that concentrates its beam on to a heating unit or boiler. Several prototype dish collectors have now been developed and can achieve temperatures of 300°C. By contrast, solar towers are much bigger and are centred in the midst of

△ Catching the Sun. Parabolic dishes turn solar radiation into electric power at the Thémis experimental plant in the French Pyrenees.

dozens, or even hundreds, of separate mirrors, which are all electronically controlled to follow the Sun's movement. Such solar towers, or furnaces, like the French experimental station at Odeillo, can heat to temperatures of more than 3,500°C.

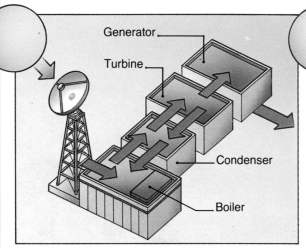

Generator

Turbine

Condenser

Boiler

△ Dish collectors focus the Sun's rays on to a boiler which produces steam. After driving the turbine, the steam is condensed back into water and is returned to the boiler.

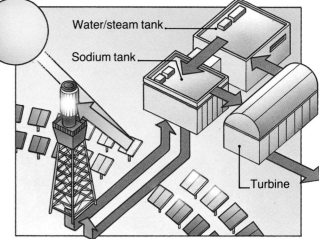

Water/steam tank

Sodium tank

Turbine

△ Hundreds of mirrors gather the Sun's rays in a solar tower. In one, in New Mexico, there are 1,775. The mirrors heat liquid sodium. This transfers the heat to turn water into steam.

⊙ POWER PANELS

In 1981, one of the world's most unusually powered aircraft crossed the Channel from France to England. The plane, Solar Challenger, was powered entirely by the rays of the Sun which were turned into electricity by photovoltaic cells that covered its wings. The flight was a dramatic demonstration of the potential of photovoltaic power panels.

Power panels have one advantage over other solar generators. They do not use an intermediate heat exchanger, such as water, to run a turbine. They have no moving parts, consume no chemicals, and need no maintenance. As a result, they can provide power for machines in remote places. But photovoltaic cells are still expensive to make. A small aircraft burning fuel could have crossed the Channel for a fraction of the cost of Solar Challenger.

△ ▽ A photovoltaic cell panel is used to provide power for a water pump in Pakistan. Below: A person works by a light which has batteries charged by sunlight.

▷ Solar cells convert only about one sixth of the energy they receive into useful electrical energy. However, many solar cells used together can make much power.

Sunlight hits a solar cell and knocks electrons across it, producing a current which is collected by the metal conductor on its surface. This conductor is linked to other cells so their power can be combined to run lights or electric pumps.

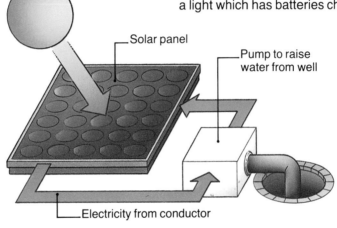

Solar panel

Pump to raise water from well

Electricity from conductor

⊙ MAKING PHOTOVOLTAIC CELLS

Ways to reduce the price of photovoltaic cells are now being sought urgently by many countries because power panels could become vital in providing power for developing remote or barren areas. One important strategy involves the search for new materials from which to build cells.

Most photovoltaic cells are still made from silicon, a substance found in rocks. During the first stage of manufacture, silicon is baked in a furnace and is then treated with various chemicals before being crystallized. Wafer-thin slices of this crystal are later cut and treated, or "doped", with special materials that react to light. When pressed together, these differently treated wafers generate electricity as light shines on them. This process is expensive, so scientists are looking at other cheaper-to-make materials, such as gallium arsenide, which also generate electricity when exposed to light.

WIND AND WAVES

No-one who has witnessed the ferocity of a gale or a storm at sea could doubt there is enormous energy in winds and waves. Indeed, for centuries, we have exploited these sources of energy, in particular, harnessing wind with mills that grind wheat and pump water.

But these machines were inefficient compared with steam and petrol engines, which have replaced them. However, modern technology is today finding new ways to develop effective wind and wave generators. In particular, scientists are exploiting new lightweight, but strong, alloys to build giant generators that can withstand 200 kph hurricane gusts and major sea storms. Such machines might one day be powerful enough to supply small towns with electricity.

△ The tidal barrage at Annapolis Royal in Canada. Each turbine can generate 18 MW of power.

▽ WIND TURBINES

Traditionally, windmills had many blades, or rotors, that were constructed of wood and canvas. These revolved at right angles to the ground and were ideal for pumping water out of the ground. However, windmill blades cannot spin round very quickly. Newly designed wind turbines have fewer, lighter blades that revolve more quickly and are better at generating power. One such wind generator has been built on Orkney, off the north coast of Scotland, and has only two giant blades. It can generate 3 megawatts of electricity, enough for a small town. Other generators have been designed to work in different ways, such as the Darrieus rotor, which has curved blades.

◉ TIDAL POWER

Extracting energy from the tides is not new. Water mills, powered by the rise and fall of the seas, were used in Europe in Norman times. However, scientists are now using the tides as a method for generating electricity. To do that, tidal generators must be built where the sea rises a considerable height so that a large volume of water can be trapped behind the generator barrage. Bays and estuaries form the best sites. One example is the Rance Estuary tidal station in Brittany where the tide rises 13.5 m.

Once the tide carries the water up the estuary, the barrage's sluice gates are closed and the trapped water is released through turbines which generate electricity. Tidal barrages can generate vast amounts of electricity in this way. However, because they are so large, they also cost a great deal of money to build.

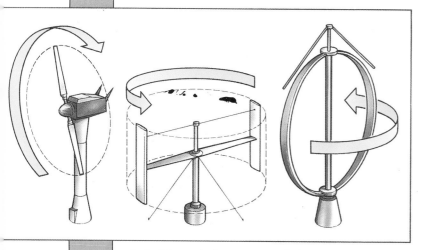

△ ▷ Most wind generators (left and photo) have blades that rotate at right angles to the ground. The Musgrove generator (middle) revolves parallel to the ground, as does the Darrieus generator.

▶ WAVE MACHINES

The seas cover most of the Earth's surface, and they are never at rest. But exploiting the ceaseless supply of energy from waves is tricky.

One particularly effective method involves the use of special buoys or towers. Open at the bottom to the sea, these allow a column of water to be trapped inside a special chamber. As waves surge up and down outside, so the water level inside the chamber goes up and down as well, forcing air through a turbine at the top of the chamber. This produces electricity. Such generators have been developed successfully in Northern Ireland, Norway and Scotland, and scientists say they will be particularly useful in providing power for navigation buoys and lighthouses in the next 5 years. Other generators use the rise and fall movements of waves to drive mechanical belts which run motors. In every case, the generators must also be made strong enough to withstand batterings from storms and gales, and the wave machines must be linked to energy stores so power is provided even when the seas are calm.

▷ ▽ The power plant built by Kvaerner Brug on an almost vertical cliff at Toftestallen in Norway, is one of the most advanced wave power generators in the world. It can generate 500 kilowatts of power. It has a chamber which fills with sea water that surges up and down in time with waves outside. This action compresses air in the chamber and forces it through a turbine.

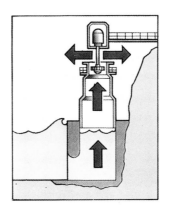
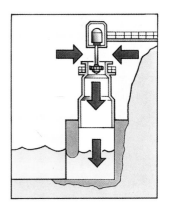

◀ OTEC

An idea for tapping the ocean's energy that was first tested in 1979 involves the exploitation of the large temperature differences between the sea's warm surface and its cold, deep water. Such a device is called an Ocean Thermal Energy Converter, or OTEC. An OTEC works by using warm surface water to evaporate a liquid, like ammonia, which has a very low boiling point. The vapour produced in this way drives a turbine which produces electricity. The cold, deep water is then pumped up to condense the ammonia vapour so that it can be used again to drive the OTEC turbines.

Ocean converters are not very efficient, however, and at present only a few have been built, like the one on the West Pacific island of Nauru. Large converters are expected to be particularly useful because, apart from making electricity, they will also pump to the surface deep water that is rich in nutrients, and which might be used to help shellfish farms.

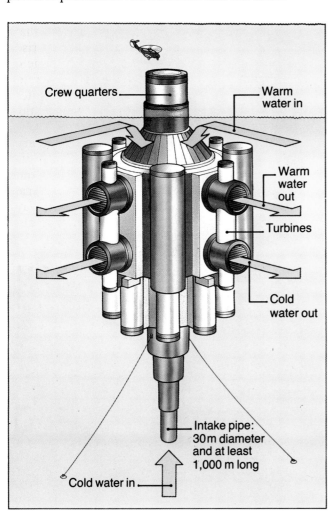

◁ Tapping the power of the deep. An OTEC works by sucking in cold, deep water. This acts as a coolant for special turbines that are driven by warm water sucked in from the ocean surface.

Crew quarters

Warm water in

Warm water out

Turbines

Cold water out

Intake pipe: 30 m diameter and at least 1,000 m long

Cold water in

THE GROUND

Deep below the Earth's surface are rocks heated to temperatures that would melt metals. This vast source of power is normally beyond our reach, except in countries where an unstable geology has brought hot rocks near the surface. One such country is New Zealand. There water, heated naturally, is used to generate 10 per cent of the nation's electricity. However, engineers are now drilling deep into the ground in order to exploit geological energy reservoirs almost anywhere in the world. Scientists claim that power generated in this way could one day become important economically, particularly in remote regions.

▼ NATURAL HOT WATER

Naturally heated water frequently bursts to the surface as geysers or hot springs. But sometimes water gets trapped below a thick layer of rock and cannot rise to the surface. When this happens, engineers drill down and pump the water up using technology for oil wells. At the surface, the pressure of the water drops and it turns to steam which drives a turbine.

Engineers face special problems when trying to build power plants based on this principle, however. In particular, natural hot water often contains impurities that corrode pipes and machinery. As a result, scientists are working to create new alloys that resist corrosion.

▼ LOCAL HEATING

Occasionally hot springs are discovered near towns and cities, as in parts of the USA, France and Japan. Then engineers can bring the water to the surface and use it directly to heat homes, rather than to drive turbines. This local heating can be very efficient. The French, for example, by 1992 hope to have 600,000 homes heated by this form of geothermal energy (from *geo* meaning Earth, and *therm* heat). Sediments in the water can build up inside pipes and block them, however. Engineers will continually have to clean equipment until scientists can develop special filters.

▽ Mining the Earth's heat. A scheme in France for heating flats with hot underground water.

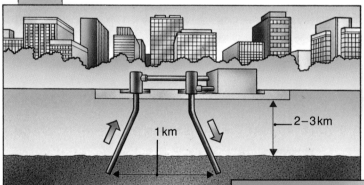

△ ▷ Making the most of heat from the deep. Bathers (right) enjoy warm waste water from a geothermal power plant in Iceland. The diagram (above) shows how hot water can be pumped from an underground spring. Cold water is pumped down to make sure the spring does not dry.

⊙ TAPPING GEYSERS

Geyser Valley in north California provides testimony to the power that can be tapped from the jets of hot water and steam that blast to the Earth's surface in some parts of the world. In the valley, among the pine trees, a series of generating plants have been built on the hills below Geyser Peak. These stations provide enough power for a city of more than one million inhabitants. Continually venting steam from below the ground, the plants give a glimpse of the awesome energy that lies beneath our feet.

Generators that make electricity from geysers operate in a similar way to those driven by natural hot water which has been artificially pumped to the surface. However, as geyser water reaches the surface, it turns to steam, of its own accord. The steam is then used to drive a turbine. The technology behind geyser generators is not new. However, scientists are trying to increase yields by searching for new sites, such as the huge geothermal reserve being developed at Beowave in Nevada, USA.

⊙ HOT DRY ROCKS

Exploiting geothermal power is relatively straightforward where natural underground water supplies are available. But often water is not present. To get round this problem scientists are developing "hot dry rock" energy plants that could be used almost anywhere. One of the first of these was built in Cornwall in southern England between 1980 and 1983. There, scientists at the Cambourne School of

△ Geysers in California, USA. These natural sources of steam are used to generate electric power for towns.

Mines drilled two wells, each 2 km deep. Then they set off underground explosions between the two wells to create a network of rock cracks, or fissures, between them. Cold water was pumped down one well. From there the water spread through the fissures to the second well, picking up heat from the surrounding rock on the way. Hot water later emerged at the second well-head. By drilling down to hotter rocks, one could get steam to run turbines.

▷ To be sure water forces its way through the underground fissures, it is pumped down at high pressure. Two rigs are needed (above). One pumps the water down, the other receives it after being heated as it passed through the hot rocks (right).

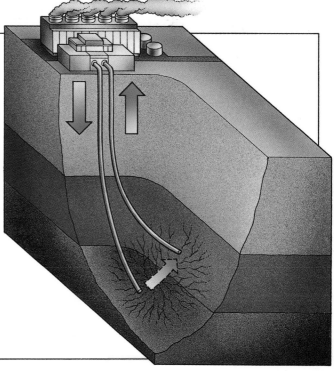

15

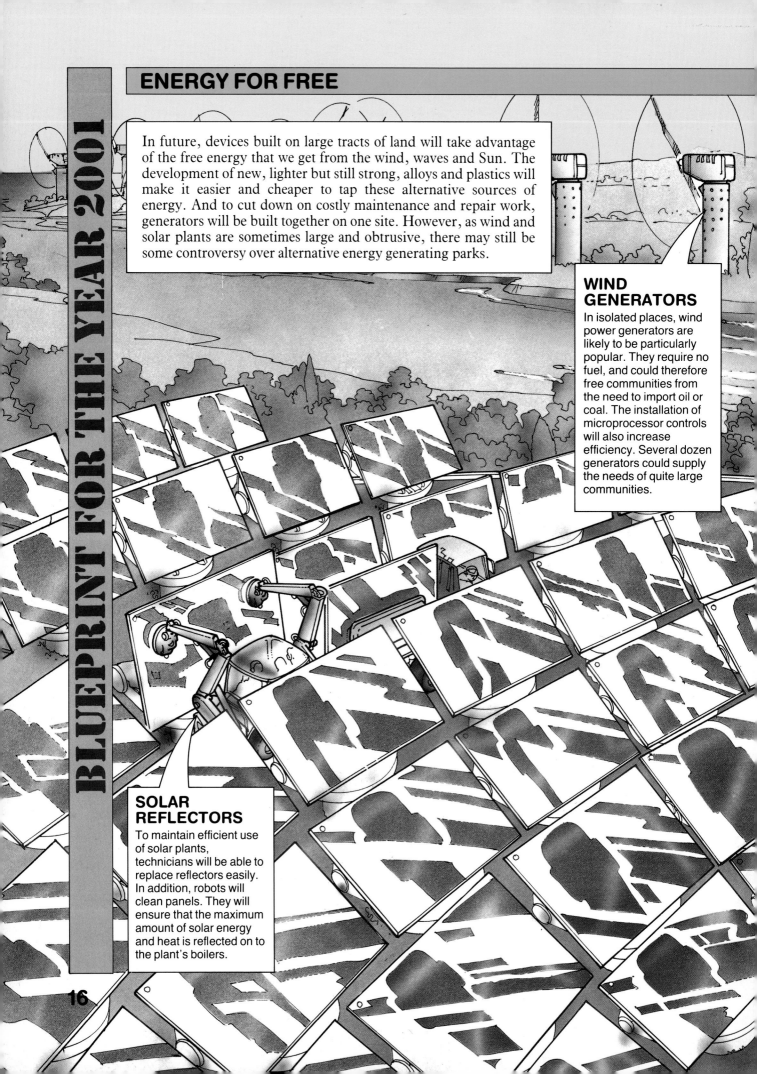

ENERGY FOR FREE

In future, devices built on large tracts of land will take advantage of the free energy that we get from the wind, waves and Sun. The development of new, lighter but still strong, alloys and plastics will make it easier and cheaper to tap these alternative sources of energy. And to cut down on costly maintenance and repair work, generators will be built together on one site. However, as wind and solar plants are sometimes large and obtrusive, there may still be some controversy over alternative energy generating parks.

WIND GENERATORS

In isolated places, wind power generators are likely to be particularly popular. They require no fuel, and could therefore free communities from the need to import oil or coal. The installation of microprocessor controls will also increase efficiency. Several dozen generators could supply the needs of quite large communities.

SOLAR REFLECTORS

To maintain efficient use of solar plants, technicians will be able to replace reflectors easily. In addition, robots will clean panels. They will ensure that the maximum amount of solar energy and heat is reflected on to the plant's boilers.

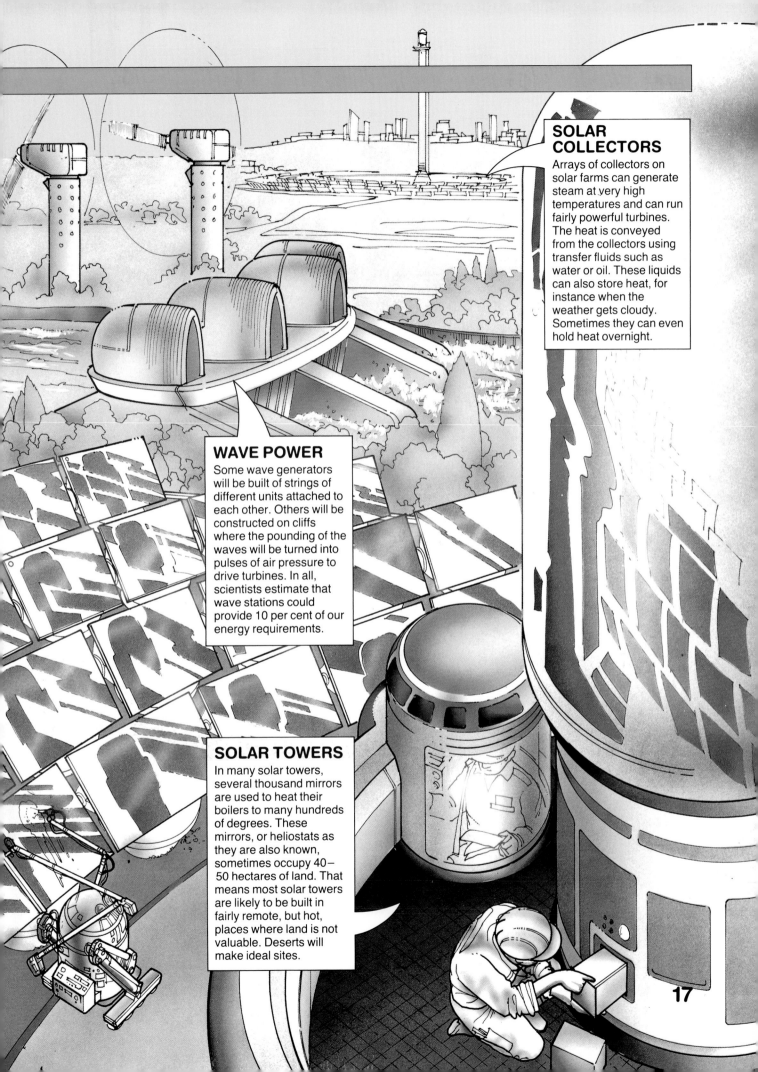

SOLAR COLLECTORS

Arrays of collectors on solar farms can generate steam at very high temperatures and can run fairly powerful turbines. The heat is conveyed from the collectors using transfer fluids such as water or oil. These liquids can also store heat, for instance when the weather gets cloudy. Sometimes they can even hold heat overnight.

WAVE POWER

Some wave generators will be built of strings of different units attached to each other. Others will be constructed on cliffs where the pounding of the waves will be turned into pulses of air pressure to drive turbines. In all, scientists estimate that wave stations could provide 10 per cent of our energy requirements.

SOLAR TOWERS

In many solar towers, several thousand mirrors are used to heat their boilers to many hundreds of degrees. These mirrors, or heliostats as they are also known, sometimes occupy 40–50 hectares of land. That means most solar towers are likely to be built in fairly remote, but hot, places where land is not valuable. Deserts will make ideal sites.

OIL AND GAS

No source of energy has had such a dramatic impact on the world as oil. It was hardly used 100 years ago. Today oil provides 38 per cent of the world's energy.

Oil has become popular because it is a liquid and can easily be transported in tankers and via pipelines. It is also light enough to be carred as fuel for cars and aircraft. Crude oil can even be made into plastics and tars. But dependence on this "black gold" may be dangerous. Oil deposits – formed millions of years ago out of the remains of prehistoric plants and animals – may soon run out. Every day, 30 million barrels are burned. Supplies may last only to 2050.

As a result, engineers have developed new technologies to obtain oil even in remote and dangerous places, for example in the frozen wastes of Siberia and Alaska, and on the seabed. They have also turned to other sources, such as shale, to maintain supplies. In addition, underground natural gas has also become an important fuel.

▼ FINDING NEW SOURCES

Exploiting previously uneconomic fields has become an important commercial priority for companies searching for new sources of oil. One solution is to build a ship that can be both a production platform and a tanker. The Canadian-built *Joides Resolution* can do this. It receives oil by lowering pipes to a well-head already installed on the seabed, and stays in position over this one spot in gales and storms by using side-thrusters as well as forward and reverse propellers. Such ships may be ideal for exploiting fields thought to be too small to merit the installation of oil platforms.

Other ideas include one device known as a

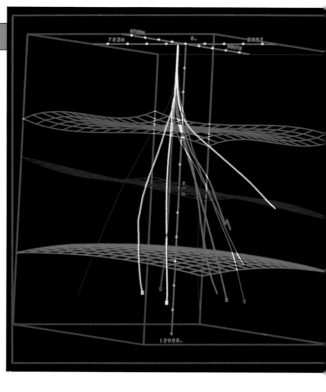

△ Teleco Drilltech in the USA use computers to create 3-D graphics of potential drilling sites.

"sniffing pig". This is the brainchild of scientists at the University of Manchester Institute of Science and Technology, England, and relies on chemical sensors that detect oil molecules in gases escaping from underwater rocks.

▷ A portable floating production platform which can act as a tanker and can move from well to well.

▽ A complete oil rig set up including remote manifolds and tension leg platforms.

Drilling rig

Filling tower

Storage tanks

Subsea remote manifold

⊳ TAR SANDS

Not all the world's oil supplies are easily pumped to the Earth's surface. Some deposits are made up of heavy types of oil which have to be obtained in special ways. Tar sands – mixtures of oil and sandstones – are a particularly important variety.

The only effective way to extract a tar sand is to strip-mine it, and this is an expensive and laborious process. The tar sand is dug up using giant mechanical scoops and the tar separated from the sand by mixing it with hot water and steam. Further processing is then needed to turn the tar into an oil fluid enough to flow through pipelines. At least 2 tonnes of tar sand have to be dug up to produce one barrel (159 litres) of oil, and much air pollution is produced.

So far, only Canada has gone ahead with major tar sands mining projects. At Athabasca in Alberta, Suncor and Syncrude, two Canadian oil companies, operate plants that produce 130,000 barrels of oil a day, a tenth of Canada's needs. But oil prices have dropped over the past decade, making tar sands plants less economic; the projects have stopped.

⊽ SHALE OIL

Shale is a slate-coloured rock rich in an oil that burns easily. There was a flourishing shale industry in Scotland in 1850, and the Ute Indians in the USA simply called it "the rock that burns". Now oil companies believe they may be able to exploit shale as an important source of energy. The most enthusiastic company is Exxon, which is developing a $3 billion shale plant at Colony, in Colorado, where shale seams are mined and oil extracted. However, plants like Colony produce massive amounts of a black, powder waste that must be stored in spoil heaps.

▽ Chunks of shale from the Colorado mine. The thin black layers of oil are sandwiched between rock debris.

△ ▽ Tar sands are usually mined with scoops (above), but the oil can be pumped up with steam (below).

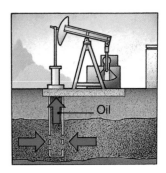

⊽ GAS FROM THE EARTH'S CENTRE

One unusual attempt to drill for natural gas is being made in Sweden. There engineers are trying to obtain gas from the centre of the Earth. Most scientists agree that gas was formed aeons ago out of decayed plants and animals. But some researchers believe this theory does not account for all the world's supplies. They think vast gas-fields, mainly of methane, were trapped deep below the Earth's surface during the planet's early history. Over the centuries, some of this gas has moved upwards. But no one has yet located "non-biological" gas.

▽ Workers at Siljan help prepare a well that is being drilled deep in an old meteorite crater. The Swedes hope to find methane 6 to 9 km below the surface.

COAL

We have used coal as an energy source for more than 2,000 years. Roman soldiers even burned it to keep warm in the cold north. However, it was not until the 18th century that coal became important, when it powered the Industrial Revolution. Coal supplied the heat that made the steam to drive the factories and trains.

Coal was formed, like oil, out of plants and animals which thrived in sunlight that shone millions of years ago. (This is why coal and oil are called fossil fuels.) When we burn coal today we release that ancient solar energy. But coal is dirty and dangerous to mine, so scientists are trying to improve mining machinery and make coal easier to handle.

▼ COMPUTERS IN CONTROL

Drilling for coal used to be a haphazard process. Today, computer-controlled electronic guiders, attached to coal cutting machines, are overcoming the problem. The guiders transmit signals to the mine's control room on the surface giving the machine's exact position. Engineers can then guide the coal-cutter to the most promising seams of coal which they have selected using data from automatic geological probes. Sensors in other parts of the mine tell the control-room computer about the condition of the coal being mined, and warn if there is a danger of fire. Other sensors measure vibration and noise and tell engineers if equipment needs replacing.

▼ NEW COAL CUTTERS

Working on a coal face is difficult. New types of equipment may make mining easier and cheaper. This may encourage the reopening of old mines at present uneconomical to work.

One development involves the use of jets of water that operate at pressures 700 times greater than normal. These jets blast out part of the coal face and are used in conjunction with traditional drills. By cutting up part of the coal face, the jets speed up the extraction process and increase the lifetime of drill heads.

▷ ▽ A "roadheader" coal drill (right) made in Glasgow, Scotland, uses water jets to help its main cutters. in long wall mining (below), coal is ripped from the seam face by a rotating cutter and removed by conveyer. Water jets suppress coal dust.

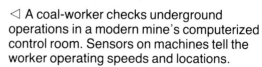

◁ A coal-worker checks underground operations in a modern mine's computerized control room. Sensors on machines tell the worker operating speeds and locations.

△ A plant in the USA for turning coal into methane gas.

▼ NEW STATES OF COAL

Coal is awkward to handle. But scientists have developed an answer to this problem. They have mixed powdered coal with water in the proportions of seven parts coal to three parts water. The mixture burns and gives off almost as much heat as solid fuel. First coal is pulverized and then mixed with water. The mixture flows as a thick liquid which can be pumped through pipes and carried in tankers like oil. Special chemical additives help to keep it flowing. In combustion chambers, the coal-and-water liquid is sprayed as fine droplets, mixed with air, ignited, and burned. Only small amounts of ash are left behind.

◄ COAL GASIFICATION

Turning coal into gas will be an important way of meeting our energy requirements in the next decade. Our present natural gas reserves will soon run out, but coal will still be with us for several hundred years. As a result, engineers are designing new, efficient coal gasification plants. Coal is fed into the top of a furnace while pressurized oxygen and steam are blown in at the bottom. A chemical reaction takes place and hydrogen and carbon monoxide are produced. These two gases are then passed over a special catalyst which helps them to react and form natural gas. The whole process is very efficient, little energy is wasted, and an easily used fuel, gas, is created. The only waste product is slag, a gritty, black glass.

Scientists have even more ambitious plans for coal gasification, however. Instead of mining coal, bringing it to the surface and then using it in power stations, they want to turn it into gas underground. One project has already been launched. By drilling holes in seams at a mine at Tono near Seattle, USA, and then pumping in steam and gas, scientists hope to produce gas that can be piped to the surface.

◁ △ This could be the coal delivery truck of the future (left), delivering liquidized coal which is pumped by hose into houses fitted with special "Coalflow" boilers. Liquid coal is poured into a beaker as part of a laboratory experiment (above).

NUCLEAR POWER

Energy is produced in reactors by splitting the heart, or nucleus, of atoms, the tiny particles of which matter is made. This is difficult to do with atoms of most chemicals. However, the atoms of a heavy metal called uranium 235 are different. They can be made to split by a process called fission. Vast amounts of energy can be released during fission. However, controlling this release is vital because many dangerous, radioactive substances are also produced. For this reason, engineers are trying to make nuclear plants safer and more reliable.

▼ FAST BREEDER REACTORS

The basic fuel of reactors is uranium. One day, the world will run out of uranium, just as it will with oil and coal, although this will not happen for several hundred years. Nevertheless, scientists are already building reactors that actually make more fuel than they consume. Such plants are called fast breeder reactors. To build one, a blanket of uranium 238, which is not fissile, is wrapped round the reactor core. The core produces heat and also very energetic atomic particles that slowly turn the uranium into plutonium, which can be burned in other types of nuclear reactor.

Only small prototype fast breeders have been built so far, one at Dounreay in Scotland, and a newer, bigger one at Creys-Melville in France. Neither makes electricity cheaply. And the plutonium can be used for nuclear bombs.

▼ ROBOTS IN REACTORS

Nuclear plants are dangerous places. Reactors produce radiation, invisible particles and rays that can cause cancer and death. Operators must be protected from these. To do this, scientists are developing "operator" robots.

▽ Workers at British Nuclear Fuel's reprocessing plant at Sellafield use robot arms to remove highly radioactive spent nuclear fuel from its cannisters.

△ Creys-Melville Fast Breeder

▽ The fast breeder reactor uses sodium to remove the intense heat which its core produces. This hot, liquid sodium is pumped into a heat exchanger to heat a separate cycle of sodium. This second sodium cycle is uncontaminated with radiation and is used to heat water to make steam that drives a turbine.

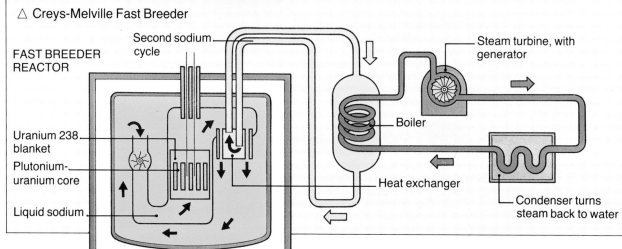

FAST BREEDER REACTOR

Second sodium cycle

Steam turbine, with generator

Boiler

Uranium 238 blanket

Plutonium-uranium core

Liquid sodium

Heat exchanger

Condenser turns steam back to water

One device, a robotic arm, has been built by the company Taylor Hitec of Chorley, England. The arm, which has many flexible sections, can slide through a hole in the casing of a reactor. Once inside, it unfolds like a telescope with joints.

Other robots have been developed to move about on wheels, or tracks, and to transport themselves to different parts of plants to carry out maintenance or inspection work. One such robot, called a Remote Reconnaissance Vehicle (RRV), was built by engineers at Carnegie-Mellon University in Pittsburgh, USA, to help clean up the contaminated nuclear plant at Three Mile Island. Robots like the RRV only work under instruction from human operators. They guide the robots using video cameras. Scientists are now developing robots to carry out tasks independently.

△ Pellets of uranium and plutonium fuel are piled up in steel tubes inside the core of the French fast breeder reactor, Super-Phenix. More than 100,000 pellets are used in the reactor.

⊙ RESEARCHING FOR SAFETY

The engineers who build nuclear power plants install many devices to make sure reactors operate safely. For example, they build extra pipes and sprays to supply emergency cooling. Nevertheless, these devices do break down, and allow a nuclear accident to occur like the one at Three Mile Island in the USA in 1979.

Some engineers are trying a different approach. They are attempting to build safety into a reactor's design, instead of adding it on later. One such reactor is Pius, designed by Asea-Atom in Sweden. It has a core surrounded by a reservoir of water. This water contains a chemical which absorbs the atomic particles that sustain reactions in a nuclear core. Only pressure from the pumps that drive the normal cooling systems prevents this water from flooding the core. However, if the pumps do fail, then the core is automatically flooded and its reaction is halted.

▽ Nuclear fuel rods in the Sandia National Laboratory research reactor in the USA glow blue. The effect is caused by highly energetic atomic particles travelling through the water surrounding the core.

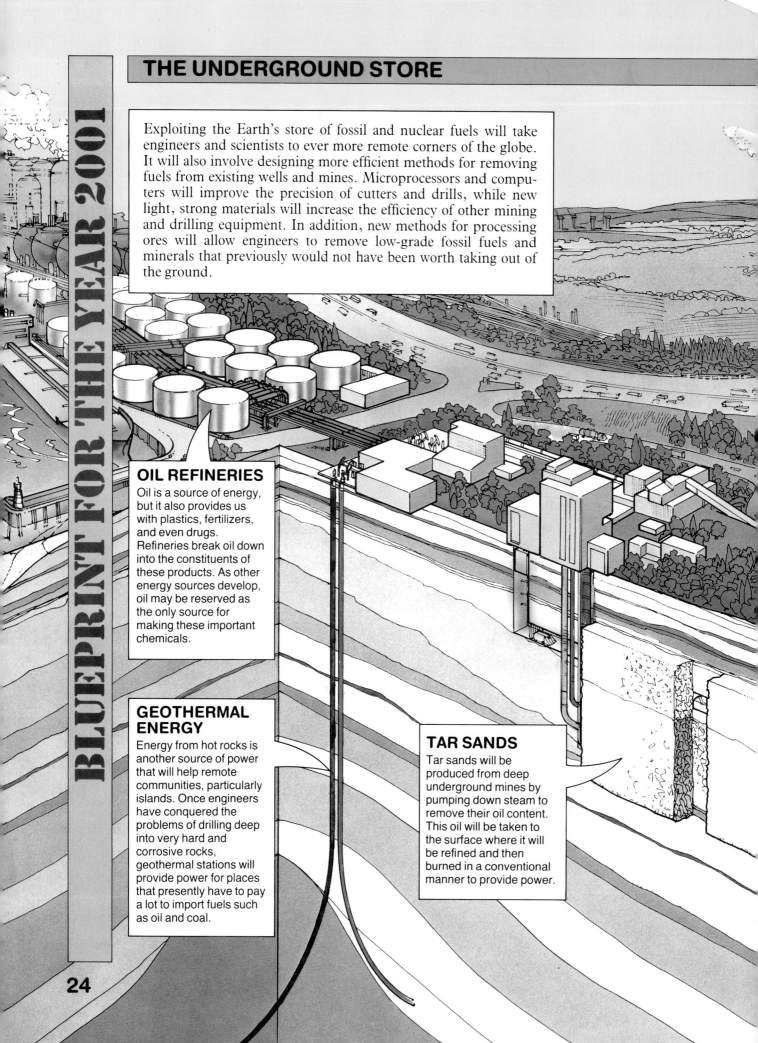

THE UNDERGROUND STORE

Exploiting the Earth's store of fossil and nuclear fuels will take engineers and scientists to ever more remote corners of the globe. It will also involve designing more efficient methods for removing fuels from existing wells and mines. Microprocessors and computers will improve the precision of cutters and drills, while new light, strong materials will increase the efficiency of other mining and drilling equipment. In addition, new methods for processing ores will allow engineers to remove low-grade fossil fuels and minerals that previously would not have been worth taking out of the ground.

OIL REFINERIES

Oil is a source of energy, but it also provides us with plastics, fertilizers, and even drugs. Refineries break oil down into the constituents of these products. As other energy sources develop, oil may be reserved as the only source for making these important chemicals.

GEOTHERMAL ENERGY

Energy from hot rocks is another source of power that will help remote communities, particularly islands. Once engineers have conquered the problems of drilling deep into very hard and corrosive rocks, geothermal stations will provide power for places that presently have to pay a lot to import fuels such as oil and coal.

TAR SANDS

Tar sands will be produced from deep underground mines by pumping down steam to remove their oil content. This oil will be taken to the surface where it will be refined and then burned in a conventional manner to provide power.

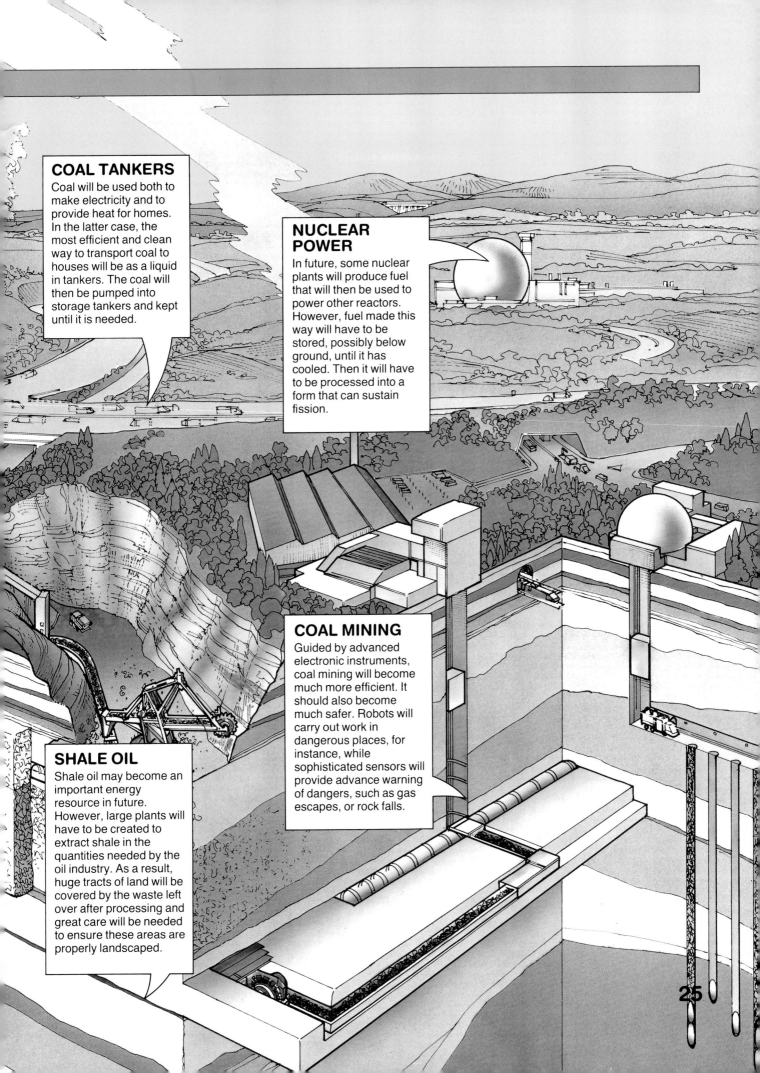

COAL TANKERS

Coal will be used both to make electricity and to provide heat for homes. In the latter case, the most efficient and clean way to transport coal to houses will be as a liquid in tankers. The coal will then be pumped into storage tankers and kept until it is needed.

NUCLEAR POWER

In future, some nuclear plants will produce fuel that will then be used to power other reactors. However, fuel made this way will have to be stored, possibly below ground, until it has cooled. Then it will have to be processed into a form that can sustain fission.

COAL MINING

Guided by advanced electronic instruments, coal mining will become much more efficient. It should also become much safer. Robots will carry out work in dangerous places, for instance, while sophisticated sensors will provide advance warning of dangers, such as gas escapes, or rock falls.

SHALE OIL

Shale oil may become an important energy resource in future. However, large plants will have to be created to extract shale in the quantities needed by the oil industry. As a result, huge tracts of land will be covered by the waste left over after processing and great care will be needed to ensure these areas are properly landscaped.

25

HIGH-COST ENERGY

Over the centuries, we have used increasingly sophisticated techniques for generating power. In the past, we burned wood and coal. Today, we use microchips and new alloys to help provide energy.

Scientists are now building powerful laser beams to generate electricity, and they use computers to carefully control fuel consumption in planes and cars. They have even built giant magnets to try to harness fusion, the nuclear fuel process which drives the Sun. If they are successful with these generators, scientists will have created a virtually inexhaustible source of energy.

Exploiting these highly sophisticated technologies is not easy, however, and only countries with a great deal of scientific expertise, and money, can make use of them.

▼ MAGNETIC CONFINEMENT

We know atoms produce heat when they break up. But they also produce energy when they join together. This process is called "fusion", and it has kept the Sun burning for billions of years. Scientists believe that if we could harness nuclear fusion it would provide the answer to all our energy problems. Its main fuel, hydrogen, a constituent of water, exists in limitless supplies. In addition, little pollution would be produced by fusion plants.

Exploiting fusion power is difficult, however. Before atoms will fuse together, they must be heated to almost 100 million°C. Controlling substances at these temperatures is very difficult. Nevertheless, scientists have come up with some answers. One has been to contain superhot atoms in powerful magnetic fields.

So far the best magnetic confinement system is Russian and is called Tokomak. It holds superhot hydrogen in a large doughnut-shaped magnetic container. A giant Tokomak, the world's most advanced fusion plant, has been built at Culham in England by a group of European nations. At present, though, it uses up more energy than it generates.

△ A technician examines one of the laser tubes that make up Nova, the giant fusion plant constructed at the Lawrence Livermore Lab.

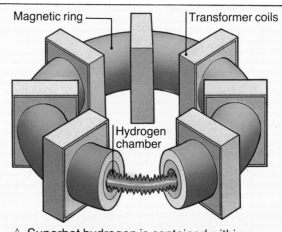

△ Superhot hydrogen is contained within a powerful magnetic field inside a Tokomak's chamber.

◖ LARGE DAM COMPLEXES

Dams are some of the world's greatest engineering feats. Brazil's Itiapu Dam, for instance, can generate as much power as a dozen large nuclear power plants and is the largest power complex on Earth. Another even bigger dam, the Three Gorges Dam, will be built on the River Yangtze in China, and will generate 25,000 megawatts of electricity, twice the Itiapu's output.

A large dam on its own can often solve a nation's energy problem by providing most of the country's electricity. Its construction also provides thousands of jobs for local people. But dams cause problems on a massive scale as well. Huge lakes form behind them flooding thousands of homes. People then have to be rehoused. These lakes also get infested. Lake Nasser at Aswan in Egypt has become a breeding ground for parasites that transmit the illness schistosomiasis (Bilharzia). In addition, a dam's turbines can become clogged with silt.

◁ Tucurui Dam in the Brazilian jungle is one of the biggest in the world.

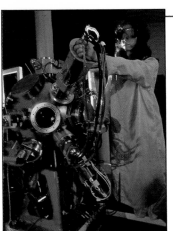

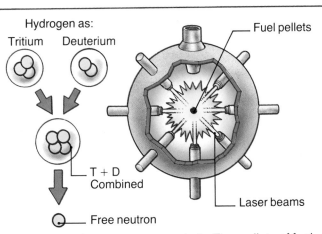

Hydrogen as:

Tritium   Deuterium

T + D Combined

Free neutron

Fuel pellets

Laser beams

△ A view into the nuclear fusion plant at the Lawrence Livermore Laboratory in the USA. The blue haze is caused by superhot hydrogen in the reactor.

△ ▷ Tiny pellets of fuel are blasted by laser inside a fusion reactor.

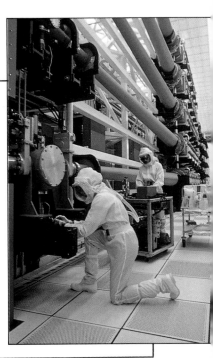

◉ LASER POWER

Scientists are working on other ways to harness fusion energy. In particular, they are using powerful lasers to blast hydrogen to extremely high temperatures and pressures. One of the biggest machines built for this purpose is called Nova. It has been constructed at the Lawrence Livermore Laboratory, in California. Nova consists of a series of extremely powerful lasers that are focused into a chamber. A tiny pellet of a special form of hydrogen fuel is then placed inside and bombarded with the laser beams. The beams not only heat the fuel but also boil off the outside of the pellet, forcing it to collapse on itself. This forces the atoms together so that they fuse.

Laser fusion shows great promise. Nevertheless, there are drawbacks. The amount of energy released from a pellet is small, and so, to produce enough power, the whole bombardment process has to be repeated – about a million times a day! Lasers are also extremely inefficient.

LOW TECHNOLOGY

The world is desperate for energy. We need energy to keep our transport systems running, our factories working, and our houses warm. In the West, people rely on large generating plants, such as coal stations. However, poor countries in Asia or Africa cannot afford the millions of pounds needed for individual plants. Scientists are now developing appropriate, small-scale methods for generating power.

Most of this "low technology" is designed to exploit a country's natural resources. For instance, small hydro-electric plants are useful in countries that have high mountains and fast-flowing streams, while in sunny, hot lands, solar-power plants can be built. In each case, the crucial factors are simplicity of construction and low cost of operation.

▶ PELTON WHEELS

The Pelton wheel is a type of waterwheel invented in Britain in the 19th century. Engineers now believe it may have a valuable future in generating power in many different parts of the globe.

The Pelton wheel has 30 or so bucket-shaped cups mounted round its rim. It is spun by jets of water that strike these cups at right angles. In this way the maximum force of the water is taken up by the wheel, which spins at very high speed as a result. Quite small streams can be used to drive a Pelton wheel and make electric-

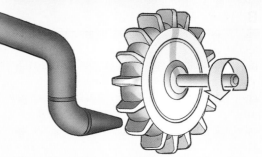

△ The Pelton wheel is very efficient at generating electricity. Even a small one that has only a 10 cm diameter can produce more than a kilowatt of power.

ity. But the stream must be flowing quite strongly to make proper use of the wheel.

Pelton wheels are ideal for generating electricity in remote places. They are long-lasting, highly efficient, and economical for small-scale use. Even relatively large ones have been used successfully. For instance, the North of Scotland Hydro-Electric Board has built Pelton wheels for some of its dams. Each is capable of generating enough electricity for a village.

◀ SOLAR PONDS

Solar ponds are used to trap the Sun's heat. The artificial pond has sloping sides and a flat bottom that is painted black. It is filled with salt water, which absorbs heat well. The water becomes very salty at the bottom, and forms a distinct layer. This becomes hot as the salt absorbs more heat than other parts of the pond.

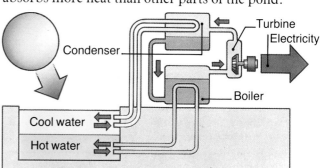

△ Israel is an ideal country for building solar ponds. It has lots of sunshine and salty lakes such as the Dead Sea.

The hot salt water is then pumped to a boiler where it is used to drive a turbine that then makes electricity. Some of the leading developers of solar ponds are based in Israel. Several pilot plants have already been built on the shores of the Dead Sea, for instance. These can each generate 150 kilowatts of power. However, in a few years, it is expected that 50 mega-watt solar ponds will be constructed there.

▶ BIOGAS

The gas given off when dung and other agricultural wastes decay is called biogas. It is a mixture of methane and carbon dioxide, and is burned for heat and power in developing countries.

When biogas is burned, it releases two-thirds as much energy as natural gas. Biogas is difficult to store, though, and so it is usually used as it is produced. This restricts its use to places such as farms. One farm in Suffolk, England, for instance, has a plant that converts pig slurry into methane. The gas is then burned in a specially converted old Ford Cortina car engine to make electricity. In China, 7 million biogas units have recently been installed.

Dung is broken down into biogas by tiny, invisible organisms called bacteria. Scientists are now searching to find new, more efficient kinds of these microscopic creatures to improve biogas output.

△ Biogas plants produce cooking gas for more than 20 million people in China. They use human waste, animal manure and agricultural residues as their basic fuel.

◁ A gas plant, built by Kaplan Industries in the USA, which uses cow manure as fuel. Bacteria break down the dung to make methane.

▷ In the USA, more than 30 large plants extract gas from pits and quarries that have been filled with refuse, like this one at Puente Hills, USA.

▶ WASTE BURNING

Every year, the world produces billions of tonnes of rubbish. Usually the waste is dumped and then covered over with soil. But landfill sites are costly to buy, so scientists are looking at ways of making good use of rubbish. One interesting idea has been to burn it to make steam which can drive a turbine and so produce electricity. A city the size of Frankfurt, which has 630,000 inhabitants, produces more than 150,000 tonnes of rubbish a year. Burning that could

provide the city with 10 per cent of its heating needs, or it could be used to generate power and cut electricity bills.

Running a waste power plant is not necessarily a straightforward business. Firstly, if the plant was to break down, then smelly, rotting rubbish would quickly mount up in city streets. However, prototype plants have so far been very reliable and have not broken down. Secondly, operators face a choice over pre-treating rubbish. Some simply shovel it into their incinerators in an untreated form. Others pre-treat it to ensure that it burns evenly and efficiently, although this process adds to running costs.

29

NEW FUELS

Most new energy sources currently under investigation are those for making electricity, and usually involve the construction of giant generating plants. However, new portable energy sources will also be needed to provide fuel for cars and buses of the 1990s and beyond. As is already clear, the world's oil supplies, from which we obtain petrol, will soon run dry.

Taking up the challenge, scientists are trying to develop new, efficient, lightweight power packs. Some are working on research on batteries that could soon be used to run electric cars. Others are developing new liquid fuels that could replace petrol. One particularly promising approach involves the fermenting of crops to make alcohol, which in turn could be used as a fuel for car engines.

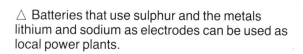

▼ ALUMINIUM BATTERIES

One solution to the world's impending petrol shortage may be provided by aluminium batteries. These rely on a reaction between oxygen in the air and aluminium to generate electricity. Aluminium batteries generate about five times the energy that is released by normal zinc batteries.

One US company, Alupower, from New Jersey, has already begun to sell aluminium batteries which are used to run small electric cars. The cars can cruise at 65 kph for up to 320 km. However, these cars are small and light, and at present have only limited uses as motorized golf buggies or maintenance vehicles for factories. Aluminium batteries are also more expensive than zinc batteries to manufacture.

△ Batteries that use sulphur and the metals lithium and sodium as electrodes can be used as local power plants.

◓ FUEL CELLS

Fuel cells operate in a simple way. Each has two plates (electrodes) that are bathed in phosphoric acid. Hydrogen, derived from other gases such as methane, is bubbled into the acid. Each hydrogen atom gives up an electron and thereby generates a current that emerges from the electrodes. The hydrogen also combines with oxygen in the acid and produces the fuel cell's only by-products: heat and water. And as fuel cells require no intermediary device, such as a turbine, to create electricity, they are up to three times more efficient than standard power plants.

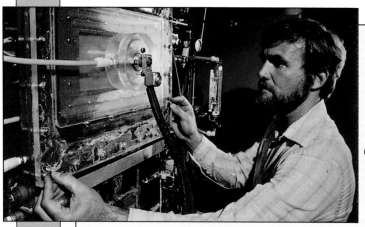

△ A US government researcher tests an experimental aluminium battery. These batteries are light and can run for many hours.

△ The Voltek car. Built by the Illinois engineering company Voltek in 1987, the electric car was built to demonstrate the advantages of aluminium batteries.

The lightness, efficiency and cleanliness of fuel cells has made them popular for use in aircraft and for various military uses. NASA has also used them on board the space shuttle. However, building large-scale versions that could provide power for communities has not been so easy. In the USA, United Technologies have attempted to build a 5 megawatt fuel cell. But fears about possible fuel spillage have caused long delays to the project.

▼ SUNFLOWER FUEL

Look at the shelves of your local supermarket. You will see bottles of oils extracted from plants – maize, soya beans, olives and sunflowers. These oils are used for cooking and are considered to be healthier than other fats such as butter. But vegetable oils may soon have another use – as fuels.

Scientists have found that oils such as sunflower oil have several advantages over other fuels. For one thing, they come from plants that are simple to grow. The oil is also easy to extract. Squeezing the plants is sufficient. In addition, it has been found that vegetable oils release 90 per cent as much energy as does standard diesel oil. However, vegetable oils also produce more carbon when they burn. This blocks up engines. One solution, perfected at the National Institute of Technology in Rio de Janeiro, has been to mix diesel and vegetable oils together. Buses in the city have successfully run on these mixtures.

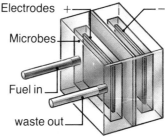

△ ▷ Bug power. 1 cc of microbial fuel contains 100 billion bacteria. Fuel is fed into the battery and waste removed. Electricity flows between the electrodes.

▲ MICROBE POWER

Using bacteria to generate electricity sounds like science fiction. Yet researchers in several countries are now working on the creation of microbial batteries. In fact, it has been known for 200 years that living beings produce tiny amounts of electricity. Now scientists based at King's College, London, have found how to exploit this phenomenon. They have discovered that electrons are released by bacteria as they break down foodstuffs such as carbohydrates: (Electricity is created by the movement of electrons.) So far, the scientists have only been able to create small microbial batteries which feed on sugar and similar substances.

▷ In Zimbabwe, sunflowers are grown (above) and oil is extracted from them. The sunflower oil is used to run farm machines such as tractors.

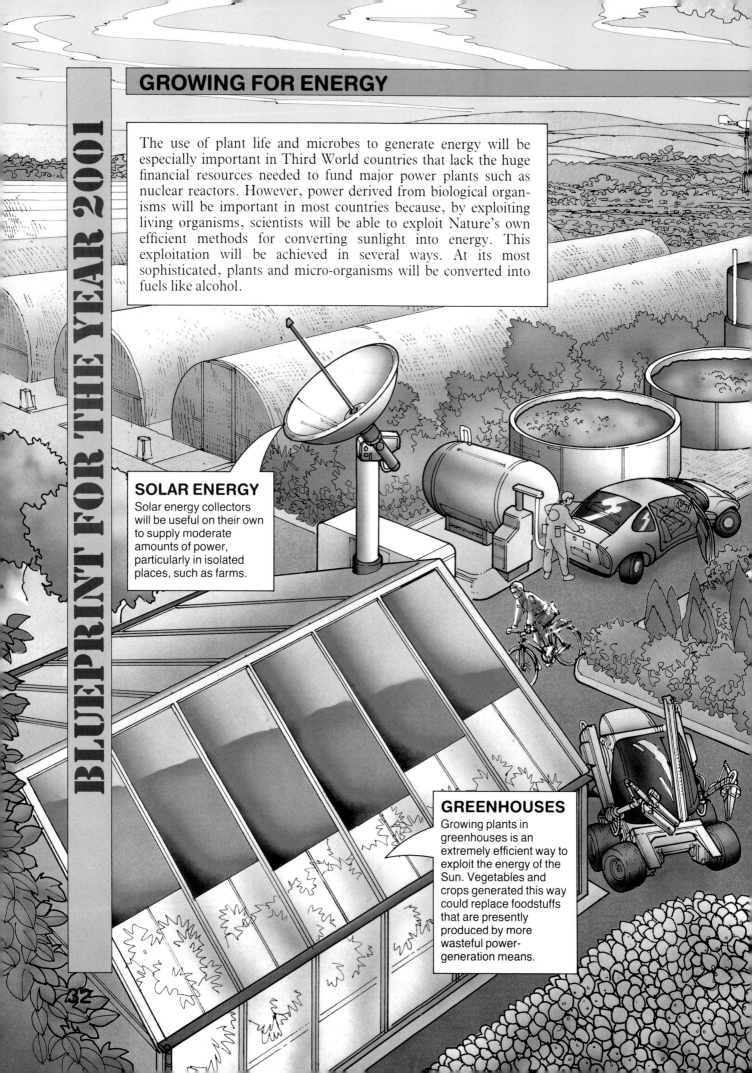

GROWING FOR ENERGY

The use of plant life and microbes to generate energy will be especially important in Third World countries that lack the huge financial resources needed to fund major power plants such as nuclear reactors. However, power derived from biological organisms will be important in most countries because, by exploiting living organisms, scientists will be able to exploit Nature's own efficient methods for converting sunlight into energy. This exploitation will be achieved in several ways. At its most sophisticated, plants and micro-organisms will be converted into fuels like alcohol.

SOLAR ENERGY
Solar energy collectors will be useful on their own to supply moderate amounts of power, particularly in isolated places, such as farms.

GREENHOUSES
Growing plants in greenhouses is an extremely efficient way to exploit the energy of the Sun. Vegetables and crops generated this way could replace foodstuffs that are presently produced by more wasteful power-generation means.

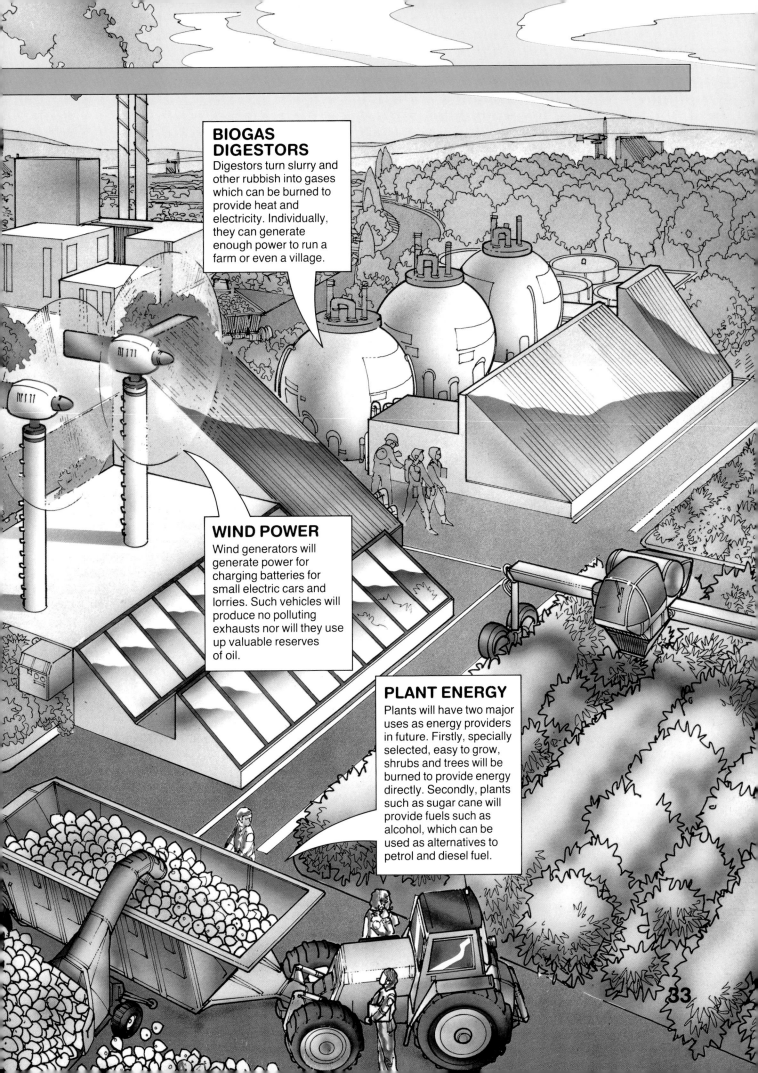

BIOGAS DIGESTORS

Digestors turn slurry and other rubbish into gases which can be burned to provide heat and electricity. Individually, they can generate enough power to run a farm or even a village.

WIND POWER

Wind generators will generate power for charging batteries for small electric cars and lorries. Such vehicles will produce no polluting exhausts nor will they use up valuable reserves of oil.

PLANT ENERGY

Plants will have two major uses as energy providers in future. Firstly, specially selected, easy to grow, shrubs and trees will be burned to provide energy directly. Secondly, plants such as sugar cane will provide fuels such as alcohol, which can be used as alternatives to petrol and diesel fuel.

POLLUTION AND CONTROL

Burning fossil fuels is still the world's main source of energy. However, it produces undesirable side-effects. Firstly, carbon dioxide is released into the atmosphere and this traps heat from sunlight. Every hour, 500,000 tonnes of carbon are burned by power stations and fossil fuel plants. Now scientists fear carbon dioxide is causing temperatures to rise across the globe. This is known as the "greenhouse effect", and it could trigger the melting of ice caps and subsequent flooding.

In addition, oil and coal power plants produce acidic oxides of sulphur and nitrogen. These gases dissolve in the clouds and later fall as acid rain, which damages trees and pollutes lakes, killing fish. Oil spills from tankers can also cause widespread death to sea life.

Countering all these environmental problems is now a major priority for scientists.

⟱ ACID RAIN

Acid rain has already been blamed for killing fish and other aquatic life in lakes and rivers in Canada, Sweden and the USA. It is also believed to be stunting the growth of trees, upsetting the nutrient content of soil, and eroding the brick- and stone-work of buildings in many parts of Europe.

Now scientists are experimenting with various techniques in a bid to block the worst effects of acid rain. In the USA, for instance, electron beams are being used to chemically activate sulphur and nitrogen oxides so that they readily combine with ammonia to produce compounds that can be used as fertilizers. In Europe, power stations are washing coal before it is burnt to remove sulphur deposits.

▷ A forester compares healthy (large) and acid rain-damaged (small) branches of spruce trees.

⊙ OIL SPILLS

In November 1986, the tanker *Kowloon Bridge* sank off the coast of Ireland. Several months later her 1,200 tonne cargo of oil was still leaking into the sea, polluting one of the wildest and most beautiful coasts of Europe. The accident dramatically illustrated the dangers that oil spills pose to the environment. Apart from disfiguring the seashore and disrupting local tourism, spills kill thousands of sea-birds. In addition, they destroy fish, an important source of food in many countries.

The problem is now one of the most serious associated with the use of oil, and scientists are trying to find new ways to lessen the effects of major oil spills. In the past, they used detergents to clean up sites of major spills, but found that these chemicals also caused environmental damage.

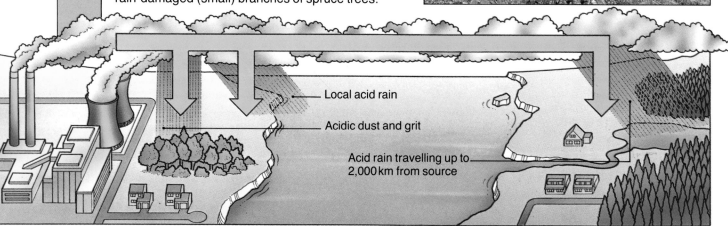

Local acid rain

Acidic dust and grit

Acid rain travelling up to 2,000 km from source

△ A Clylonet 100 is tested for effectiveness. This oil "vacuum cleaner" was designed in the USA to remove oil that has spilled over a large area of water.

△ A soil scientist working for the US Agricultural Department examines a sample of lake water while a colleague adds lime to neutralize acidity from acid rain.

One approach being followed by the French company TR Sallinger is the design of inflatable rafts each able to carry 100 cubic metres of oil. Carried to tanker wrecks on helicopters, Pollutanks, as they are called, can be prepared for use in minutes.

▼ MESOCOSMS

Assessing the exact effects of oil spills and other discharges in the oceans is very important. But it is also very difficult.

Scientists at the Marine Ecosystems Research Laboratory at the University of Rhode Island, in the USA, have come up with a solution to this problem. They have built a series of towers that are about 15 m high and 4 m in diameter. These towers are called mesocosms, which means intermediate worlds. Mesocosms are filled with sea water, fish and other marine organisms. By adding various pollutants and chemicals, the exact effects of spills can then be accurately assessed by scientists.

⊛ REPAIRING THE DAMAGE

Scientists have only recently become aware that some power plants are seriously damaging our forests, rivers, lakes, and seas. Many disagree about the exact role that oil, coal and nuclear station play in this environmental upheaval. Nevertheless, some emergency counter measures are being taken where damage has become particularly severe.

In Sweden and Norway, for instance, lakes have been sprayed with lime to offset the build up of acid rain in the water. However this does not solve the long-term problems caused by poisonous emissions from power stations. To tackle that, generating plants are being fitted with filter units which can remove oxides from their emission gases. More and more countries are fitting these. Japan, for example, has already installed almost 200 such units.

▷ Mesocosms are built near the seashore where it is easy to pump in water and sea life. In this way, an environment similar to the real one is created. Probes and monitors are fitted to the tanks before oil and other pollutants are added. From the reactions of creatures in the tanks, scientists can calculate the likely impact of spills at sea.

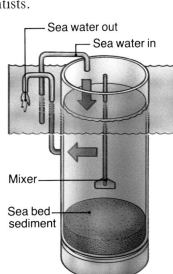

Sea water out
Sea water in
Mixer
Sea bed sediment

Just like coal and oil plants, nuclear reactors have their own unpleasant side-products. They generate radioactive waste.

When uranium atoms split, other, dangerous atoms are formed, including types of strontium, caesium and krypton. These all emit radiation. Radiation is invisible but it can be very harmful and can even kill people. Nuclear plant operators must therefore take great care about dealing with reactor waste.

Several solutions are being investigated. One involves putting nuclear waste in containers in underground caverns. Another is to place waste containers on the sea bed. However, nuclear waste can remain radioactive for thousands of years, which means it may still pose a danger to future generations. In addition, dismantling old nuclear reactors is an extremely intricate and dangerous business.

⊙ STORING WASTE

Deep below ground, scientists and engineers one day hope to find homes for their most dangerous radioactive wastes. They want to bury them in caverns a kilometre or so underground. The process is controversial because some people fear that radioactivity might escape and contaminate part of the countryside and pollute drinking water supplies. In addition, its continued safe burial is impossible to ensure.

The problem is particularly severe when dealing with high-level nuclear waste, the most dangerously radioactive kind. This type is

mostly made up of used reactor fuel. So far, the only nuclear waste put in mines, such as one at Asse, in West Germany, is of the medium-level variety, and includes material like the metal alloys used as containers for nuclear fuel inside a reactor. High-level waste is currently stored in vaults near reactors, where it can be safeguarded.

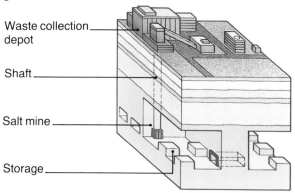

Waste collection depot

Shaft

Salt mine

Storage

△ Low-level waste from French reactors is stored in trenches at the Centre de la Manche, Normandy.

▽ One nuclear waste scheme involves the pumping of radioactive material on to the sea bed.

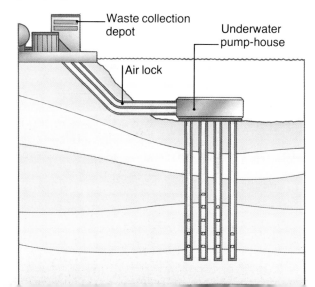

Waste collection depot

Underwater pump-house

Air lock

△ Spent fuel stored underwater temporarily.

COPING WITH ENERGY

⩩ VITRIFICATION

Vitrification involves turning highly radioactive fluid into a solid, glass-like substance. Firstly, the liquid content is boiled away, then the powdered remains mixed with pieces of glass. This mixture is heated in a stainless-steel furnace to 1,000°C so that both the waste and glass melt. The molten mixture is then poured into storage drums where it solidifies. These drums are later buried underground.

A year's waste from a 1,000 megawatt reactor would fill about seven drums and should be highly resistant to erosion from water that might spill into the underground storage caverns. However, some scientists believe that glass under constant radioactive bombardment from its waste constituents might not function normally. It could allow water to seep through to the waste. As a result, scientists have tried to turn waste into an even more stable form. They have mixed waste with metals such as calcium, compressed the mixture, and then heated it to extreme temperatures. The result is a highly water-resistant artificial radioactive rock.

⩩ DECOMMISSIONING

The first nuclear power plants were built in the mid-1950s and have operated with varying success since then. But now many reactors are coming to the end of their operating lives. The headache facing engineers is to find ways to dismantle, or decommission, them. There are three options: Reactors could be left, without fuel, as they are; concrete shells could be built over their highly radioactive cores; or their entire structures could be dismantled, their sites

△ Workers melt radioactive waste with surrounding rock and glass so that vitrification can be done on site.

levelled and the land returned to its original condition. The last option is the best for the environment. It is also the most expensive. To fully decommission a medium-sized reactor would cost at least £300 million. This figure is equivalent to a third of the total cost of constructing such reactors in the first place.

One of the few attempts that have been made at decommissioning has taken place at a small gas-cooled reactor at Sellafield in England. Experience with removing its highly radioactive components and spent fuel rods has suggested that in future greater care will have to be taken when constructing reactors.

▽ A reactor vessel is removed by workers dismantling a nuclear plant in Sweden.

▽ Heat exchangers are removed from a gas-cooled reactor at Sellafield, England.

SAVING ENERGY

Energy technology is not only concerned with producing power. There is another important way to ensure that the world will have enough energy for the 21st century – by preventing it from being wasted.

Many of our principal sources of power are inefficient, particularly oil and coal stations. Although they produce a lot of electricity, some of their energy is also given off as waste heat. One recent idea has been to use that waste heat to warm homes which have been built near power stations.

Similarly, architects are now planning houses that need less energy to keep them warm. By carefully arranging the placing of windows and doors, by insulating walls and roofs, and by double glazing windows, it has been possible to build homes that use less than average amounts of energy.

▼ SUPERCONDUCTORS

When electricity flows along ordinary wires, energy is lost as heat. Scientists have sought ways to make electricity transmission more efficient. Now they believe superconductors may provide the answer.

Superconductors are substances that do not turn any electricity into heat. Until recently, however, the only known superconductors worked at around −230°C. As a result, they required expensive cooling, which made them uneconomical. But in 1986, Karl Muller at IBM's laboratory in Zurich, Switzerland, discovered chemicals that superconducted at −170°C, a more manageable temperature.

△ Main pipes beneath roads carry hot water from CHP power stations to homes in Helsinki, Finland.

◉ COMBINED HEAT AND POWER

Most electricity is generated by turbines driven by steam that is produced from coal, oil or nuclear fuel. But at least 10 per cent of the heat used to produce steam is wasted, while only 30 per cent of a station's steam energy is turned into electricity. The rest becomes waste gas and warm water.

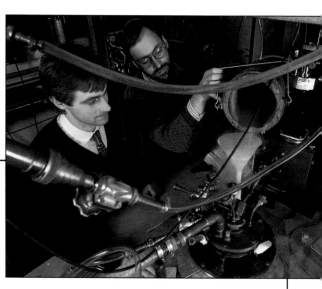

△ Cooling a superconductor with liquid-gas.
◁ In insulating materials like rubber and glass (top), electrons are tightly bound to atoms and do not flow as electric currents. In materials like metals (middle), electrons are more loosely bound. In superconductors (below) electrons are bound in pairs that move straight along wires without losing energy.

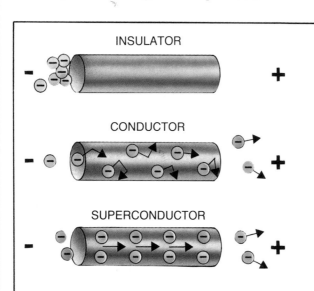

INSULATOR

CONDUCTOR

SUPERCONDUCTOR

Combined heat and power (CHP) systems exploit this normally wasted energy. To do this effectively, however, a CHP power station has to be run in a slightly unconventional way. Less electricity is generated, but the station produces waste water at much higher temperatures. The overall effect is to raise the efficiency of the power station to more than 50 per cent because of the production of this hot water, which is pumped to blocks of flats and factories. Here it is used for room and workspace heating. Money must be spent on pipes and pumps to channel this hot water, of course. Nevertheless, combined heat and power schemes have now been successfully built for homes in major European cities.

▼ ENERGY EFFICIENT HOMES

Houses that trap the Sun's rays for heat are not new. The Greeks and Romans warmed their homes this way. Now engineers are designing modern houses that are heated by the same method. They make maximum use of the Sun's rays to directly heat rooms and provide hot water. In such houses, large south-facing windows trap heat and light from the Sun. Floors and walls are made of thick bricks which retain the heat. These bricks keep the house warm at night when the temperature outside falls. In addition, windows are double-glazed to prevent heat escaping, while thick roof and wall insulation keep warm air inside the house. On the house's north side, trees give protection from the wind in winter and provide shade in summer.

▷ To get good yields of alcohol from sugar cane, special energy-rich forms of the plant are being tested, as here in Puerto Rico. They are part of a bioenergy project led by David Hall, of King's College, London.

◉ BIOENERGY

One method for improving energy efficiency on farms involves the growing of special plants. These plants are known as "catch crops" and they can be grown in fields in between main crops. They have two uses. They can either provide food or energy. The most appropriate catch crops include beet, mangels, swedes, kale, mustard and cereals such as oats, barley and rye.

Once catch crops are grown, a farmer can use them for feeding animals or people, sell them to a central agency for energy conversion, or ferment them directly into methane or other fuel. In some parts of the world major bioenergy projects have been launched, particularly in nations that lack plentiful supplies of coal or oil such as Brazil.

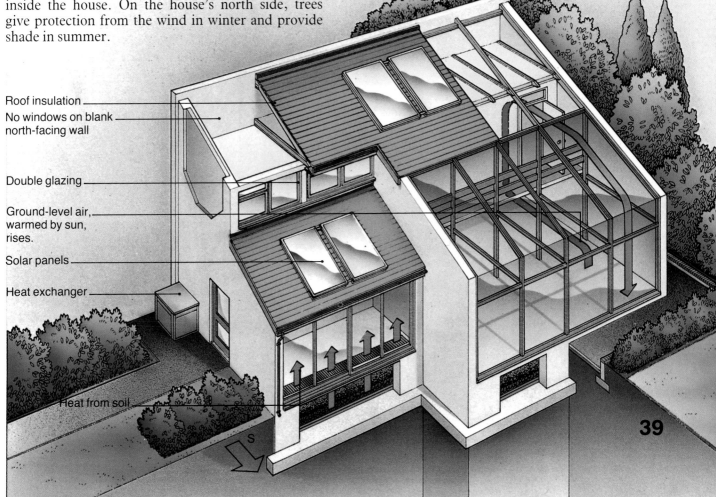

Roof insulation

No windows on blank north-facing wall

Double glazing

Ground-level air, warmed by sun, rises.

Solar panels

Heat exchanger

Heat from soil

S

39

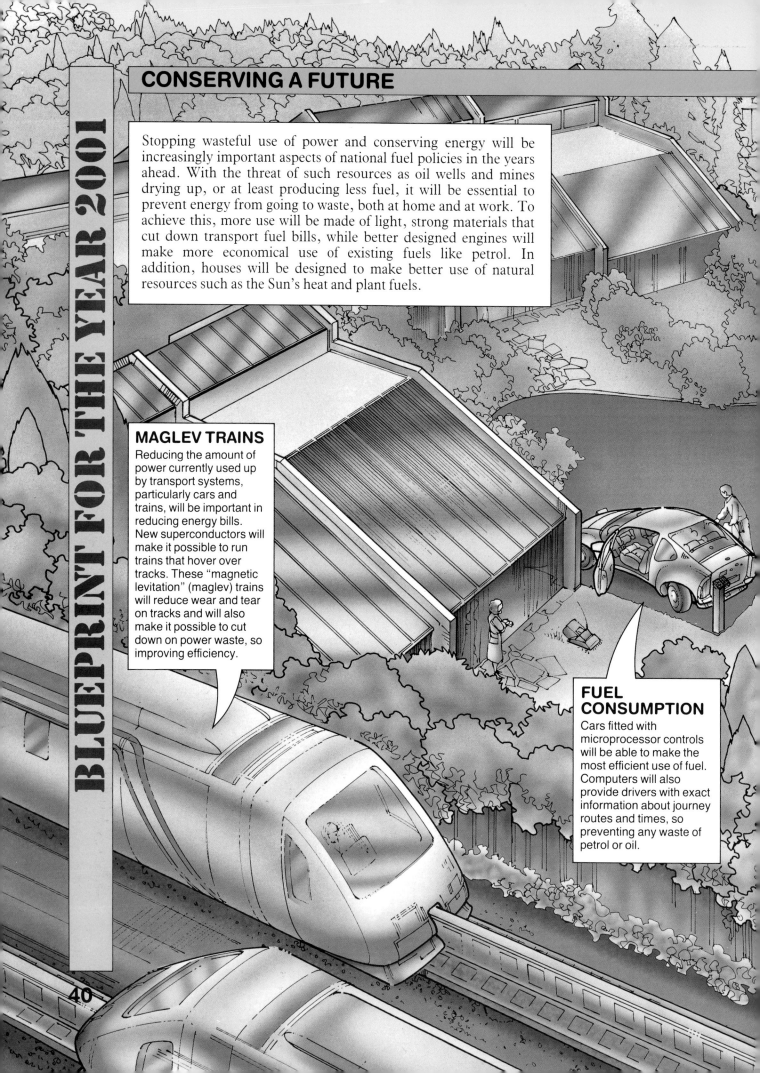

CONSERVING A FUTURE

Stopping wasteful use of power and conserving energy will be increasingly important aspects of national fuel policies in the years ahead. With the threat of such resources as oil wells and mines drying up, or at least producing less fuel, it will be essential to prevent energy from going to waste, both at home and at work. To achieve this, more use will be made of light, strong materials that cut down transport fuel bills, while better designed engines will make more economical use of existing fuels like petrol. In addition, houses will be designed to make better use of natural resources such as the Sun's heat and plant fuels.

MAGLEV TRAINS

Reducing the amount of power currently used up by transport systems, particularly cars and trains, will be important in reducing energy bills. New superconductors will make it possible to run trains that hover over tracks. These "magnetic levitation" (maglev) trains will reduce wear and tear on tracks and will also make it possible to cut down on power waste, so improving efficiency.

FUEL CONSUMPTION

Cars fitted with microprocessor controls will be able to make the most efficient use of fuel. Computers will also provide drivers with exact information about journey routes and times, so preventing any waste of petrol or oil.

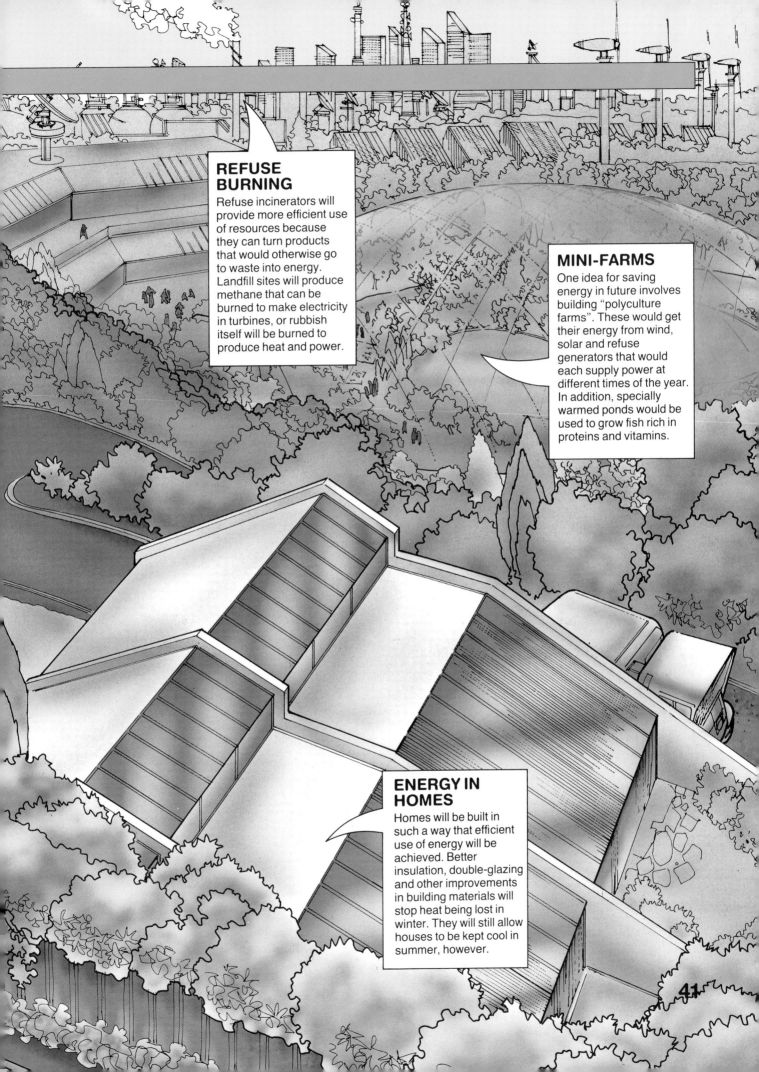

REFUSE BURNING

Refuse incinerators will provide more efficient use of resources because they can turn products that would otherwise go to waste into energy. Landfill sites will produce methane that can be burned to make electricity in turbines, or rubbish itself will be burned to produce heat and power.

MINI-FARMS

One idea for saving energy in future involves building "polyculture farms". These would get their energy from wind, solar and refuse generators that would each supply power at different times of the year. In addition, specially warmed ponds would be used to grow fish rich in proteins and vitamins.

ENERGY IN HOMES

Homes will be built in such a way that efficient use of energy will be achieved. Better insulation, double-glazing and other improvements in building materials will stop heat being lost in winter. They will still allow houses to be kept cool in summer, however.

41

NEW FRONTIERS

Microwaves beamed down to Earth

The projects described so far in this book are designed to meet our energy requirements in the next 10 years. However, the world's energy problems will not disappear after that. By the year 2000, we will need even more supplies of power to run our houses, factories, cars and planes, and some present sources of fossil fuels will start to dry up. But it is very difficult to estimate exactly how much energy we will need. Improving energy forecasts, by using powerful new computers, is therefore an important priority.

In the meantime, scientists are investigating several long-range projects which they hope might become vital in providing not only the Western world, but all countries, with power in the centuries ahead.

⊚ SOLAR SPACE STATIONS

Using giant arrays of photovoltaic cells in space is one of the most imaginative and ambitious energy schemes now being considered. The idea was first proposed by American Peter Glaser. He envisaged building orbiting stations, each made up of many square kilometres of cells. In space, the cells would be unaffected by clouds or the atmosphere, and would be highly efficient at turning solar energy into electricity. The 10,000 megawatts of power that each station would generate would then be turned into microwave beams. These beams would be transmitted to Earth and turned back into electricity. Forty-five of these stations could provide all the USA's electricity needs. But construction costs would be immense, while some fear that the stations' powerful microwave beams might badly damage the environment.

⊚ SOLAR CHIMNEYS

One unusual type of new power plant exploits two different forms of alternative energy generation: wind and solar. Created by Professor Schlaich of Stuttgart University, West Germany, a solar chimney consists of a tower 200 m high and 10 m wide. This is surrounded by a solar collector area made of plastic sheets. This heats air like a greenhouse, causing the air to enter the chimney and rise up it. In the chimney, a wind turbine is driven by the strong, rising current of air. Fresh air is sucked in from outside the collection area to keep the cycle going. A solar chimney heated this way does not require direct solar radiation, but can still generate electricity when the sky is overcast.

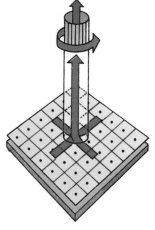

▷ △ A solar chimney is made of corrugated steel, and is surrounded by a collection area of transparent plastic (above). The clear plastic traps the Sun's heat. The air inside heats, rises and runs the turbine.

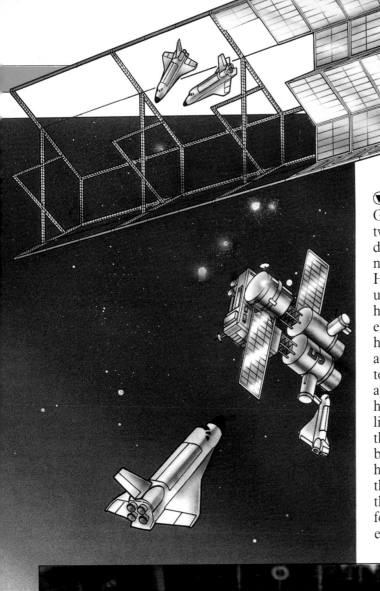

Photovoltaic cell array

▼ FUTURE FUSION

Giant magnetic fields and powerful laser beams are two of the most advanced techniques that have been developed to create the incredible temperatures needed to fuse hydrogen atoms into those of helium. However, another, strictly experimental, method uses beams of positively charged ions to compress hydrogen fuel pellets. Ions are atoms that have gained either a positive or a negative charge because they have too few, or too many, electrons. In particle accelerators, powerful electric charges are generated to attract ions of the opposite charge at speeds approaching that of light (300,000 kps). But ions have a far greater mass than photons, which transmit light, and so their beams carry much greater power than light-generated lasers. For this reason, ion beams may prove to be more effective at heating hydrogen. Scientists in Britain, West Germany and the USA have already launched ion projects. Nevertheless, ion accelerators face problems over the focussing of beams of particles that normally repel each other as they carry the same electric charge.

◁ A particle beam fusion accelerator at the Sandia National Laboratories at Albuqueque, New Mexico, lights up a web of electrical discharges. Arranged like spokes in a 22 m-wide wheel, 36 beam accelerators pulse electricity towards the centre to produce a 100 trillion watts of power for a mere 30 millionths of a second.

GLOSSARY

Alternative energy Power generation that exploits resources, such as wind, waves and Sun, that will not run out with continual use.

Atom The smallest unit of a chemical element. An atom, which has a diameter less than one ten-millionth of a millimetre, has a central nucleus of protons and neutrons around which orbits a swarm of electrons.

Battery A device for storing electrical energy.

Catalyst A substance which aids a chemical reaction but which is itself unaffected by the process.

Condenser A device that is used to cool a vapour causing it to condense to a liquid.

Coolant The liquid or gas which is pumped through a nuclear reactor to remove its heat.

District heating Heat for homes which is derived from waste energy from power stations.

Element A substance, such as oxygen, hydrogen and carbon, that cannot be reduced into simpler chemical units. There are 92 naturally occurring elements.

Energy A measure of a system's ability to do work.

Generator The part of a power station which converts mechanical energy, usually produced by pressure of steam, into electricity.

Geothermal energy The general name for energy derived from Earth's core.

Geyser A spring that discharges hot water and steam.

Grid The system by which electricity is transmitted round a country

Hydro-electric power Electricity derived from the flow of water.

Methane A naturally produced gas that can be burned for energy.

Natural gas A mixture of gases produced underground and which is used as fuel.

Nuclear fission The splitting of an atom into fragments. This produces energy.

Nuclear fusion The uniting, at very high temperatures, of the atoms of light elements. The process releases energy.

Nuclear reactor A device in which the process of nuclear fission is used to generate heat.

Power Technically, the rate at which work is done or energy is released. More generally, "power" and "energy" are often used interchangeably.

Radioactivity Changes which occur in the large atoms of elements such as uranium. When this happens nuclear radiation is released.

Turbine A machine that is used to transform mechanical energy into electricity. The mechanical energy may come from steam, water or by burning gases that spin a rotating shaft.

Uranium 235 The form of the chemical element uranium which has 143 neutrons in its nucleus and which supports nuclear fission.

Uranium 238 The form of uranium which is usually found in nature. It is transformed in fast breeder nuclear reactors into plutonium which can support nuclear fission.

Watt A unit of power. A kilowatt (kW) of electricity is required to run a small fire. A few megawatts (MW) (millions of watts) can fulfill the needs of a small community.

Watt-hour A unit of energy equal to the power of one watt operating for one hour.

INDEX